Edwin Smith

An exclusive collaboration with the RIBA British
Architectural Library Photographs Collection

© Chris Beetles Ltd 2010
8 & 10 Ryder Street
St James's
London
SW1Y 6QB

020 7839 7551
gallery@chrisbeetles.com
www.chrisbeetles.com

ISBN 978-1-905738-25-0

Written and researched by David Wootton, with an essay by Robert Elwall
Edited and designed by Giles Huxley-Parlour
Colour separation and printing by the Midas Press

Edwin Smith

Self-portrait, 1950s

A Genius Rediscovered

During the 1950s and 1960s, Edwin Smith established his reputation as one of Britain's foremost topographical and architectural photographers[1] to such an extent that an admiring John Betjeman was moved to declare him 'a genius at photography'[2]. Yet even by the time of his premature death from cancer in 1971, Smith's standing had become less assured, with many viewing his romantic, picturesque style as increasingly anachronistic in the light of the emergence of a new hard-edged school of photography more attuned to the *événements* and social turbulence of the period. Even the subsequent untiring efforts of his widow and former collaborator, Olive Cook, to promote his work were unable to arrest this fall from critical grace with the result that – until recently – he has remained largely shunned by the photographic establishment. Yet today there are signs that his photography is on the cusp of a revival.

Generously bequeathed by Olive Cook to the British Architectural Library at the Royal Institute of British Architects on her death in 2002, Edwin Smith's archive is now publicly available for the first time and has undergone an extensive programme of conservation, cataloguing, digitisation and publication. His inclusion in Tate Britain's exhibition 'How We Are: Photographing Britain from the 1840s to the Present', in 2007, represented an important further stage in his rehabilitation, and the current show at Chris Beetles Gallery – the first devoted to his work for many years – is but one indication of a burgeoning appreciation of his imagery. This appreciation has been aided by an awakening interest in the post-war decades in general and the Neo-Romantic movement in particular, a movement to which Smith's photography bears a close affinity. Above all, the themes underlying Smith's work are once again matters for impassioned cultural debate: an empathetic response to, and concern for, the preservation of the countryside and our built heritage buttressed by an unremitting antipathy to inappropriate development and the numbing standardisation that erodes subtle regional variations.

Edwin Smith was born into humble circumstances in Camden Town, London, in 1912. After an abortive attempt to forge a career as an architect, he took up photography professionally in the mid 1930s with the help and encouragement of the artist, Paul Nash, and the folk art expert, Enid Marx. While the influence of Nash was obvious in his pictures of blasted trees and the eerily contorted shapes to be found in nature, Smith's pre-war work was diverse, embracing as it did landscape, architecture, found objects, plants and flower studies, the ballet, nudes and portraits. In addition, he undertook fashion photography for the British edition of *Vogue* and advertising work for Marcus Brumwell's Stuart Advertising Agency, whose roster of artists included Edward Bawden and John Piper. The social problems of the 1930s also came before his lens, in particular with a commission from the MP, Sir Arnold Talbot Wilson, to photograph the mining, fishing and shipbuilding communities of north-east England, although the results displayed little of the reformist ardour one might have expected but instead celebrated the nobility of the working man. The less savoury mien of the decade is also revealed in the photographs recording Nazi achievements that he took on a trip to Germany.

Uniting this eclectic body of subject matter was Smith's excitement at discovering photography's possibilities and above all the revelatory light the medium could shed on the visual richness of the world he inhabited. This epiphanic quality of photography was well expressed by Smith when he wrote in 1936,

> Camera-eye has revealed a new visual sphere for my habitation; much that was before visually incomprehensible has become, in the presence of the camera, significant. A divining rod finding its own peculiar water, with myself a passive diviner. There is, of course, much still to be divined.[3]

Always in Smith's photography there is this sense of quest, an unrelenting need to explore and record the overlooked and underappreciated. Also common to his treatment of these subjects is a feel for pattern and texture as well as an eye for the incongruous.

His imagery during this period and indeed later was heavily influenced by the great French photographer, Eugène Atget (1857-1927), who from 1898 onwards painstakingly recorded the older Parisian streets and monuments that had survived the nineteenth-century 'improvements' of Baron Haussmann but were then freshly threatened by the construction of the Métro. Smith was a proud owner of a collection of Atget's images, published posthumously in 1930 under the title *Atget: Photographe de Paris*, and his delight in visual intricacies and incongruities together with his ability to discern the extraordinary in the seemingly ordinary, which remained constant refrains in his photography, owed much to his French forerunner. Nowhere is this better shown than in his largest corpus of pre-war work – that devoted to popular culture as manifested in the pub, music hall, night club and above all the circus and fairground. In contrast to those of Atget, however, which were taken on a large format camera with consequently long exposures that prevented the inclusion of people, Smith's images, captured with his smaller, more spontaneous Contax, dynamically convey the drama of performance and the crowd's excitement and apprehension. While Atget's photographs appear a poignant requiem for a world that was vanishing as swiftly as his beloved *Vieux Paris*, Smith's are a celebration of a vibrant, culture conveying not just 'the fun of the fair' and its Baroque trappings but also its skulduggery and terrors – the intensity of Smith's gaze transforms the fairground gallopers into frenzied participants in a surrealistic nightmare [Plate 1].

Edwin Smith's interest in this subject matter was doubtless stimulated by his close friendship with Enid Marx and it was heightened when, in 1943, he abandoned his wife and child to embark on what proved to be a remarkably creative and long-lasting relationship with Olive Cook (1912-2002), whom he eventually married in 1954. As well as being a gifted painter, Cook possessed a formidable intellect and boundless energy. In addition, her employment at the National Gallery had brought her into close contact with many artists such as Michael Rothenstein and John Aldridge and she was thus able greatly to widen Smith's circle of friends and contacts.

In 1945, Cook relinquished her job at the National Gallery to pursue with Smith a freelance career in painting and writing. One of the first fruits of their collaboration was their transformation of *The Saturday Book*, an idiosyncratic 'cabinet of curiosities' that appeared annually each Christmas, running for 34 issues from 1941 until 1975. Smith's first photographic contribution was to number 4 (1944), and thereafter his photographs enriched every issue, even posthumously, with Cook often writing the commentaries to the images and sometimes her own pieces. The couple also laid out their own articles and, as Leonard Russell, *The Saturday Book*'s first editor, generously acknowledged, they were 'responsible for the odd, individual and imaginative visual quality of the book'[4]. These articles inventively covered a wide variety of subjects including bicycling, embroidery, and 'Moving Pictures before the Cinematograph' but popular art, seen in studies of matchbox-top design, ships' figureheads, and most engagingly 'Beside the Seaside', and architecture, characteristically represented by studies of the offbeat such as Ferdinand Cheval's fantastical self-built home, the Palais Idéal at Hauterives, proved recurrent themes. While Smith took few pictures specifically for the magazine, merely recycling those he had in stock, *The Saturday Book* did nevertheless provide a wider audience for his imagery as well as giving him an invaluable insight into book production and layout.

If Edwin Smith's pre-war work had been interesting but essentially derivative, he developed his own distinctive photographic language during the 1950s thanks largely to a series of book commissions from the publishing firm of Thames & Hudson, which had been established in 1949 with a specific remit to engender a greater appreciation of Britain's visual, as opposed to literary, heritage. Three of the books for which Smith provided the photographs were architectural. The first, *English Parish Churches* (1952), written by the economist Graham Hutton, already reveals the hallmarks of Smith's mature style – a love of the intimate and picturesque; an empathetic response to, and conveyance of, the *genius loci*; a reverential expression of the textures of materials and the history to which they bear witness; and an unfailing ability, as Betjeman astutely observed, to 'find a significant detail in a church – an oil lamp, a bell rope, or a harmonium which would conjure up a whole parish of people'[5]. Above all, the book – which broke new ground in seeking photographically to suggest how worshippers express their faith through architecture, artefacts and the diurnal trappings of church life – was an eloquent testimony to Smith's declaration that for him photographing in a good village church was 'unalloyed bliss'[6]. A similar enthusiasm underpinned *English Abbeys and Priories* (1960).

The preservationist aims that were muted in these two works on ecclesiastical subjects burst to the fore in *English Cottages and Farmhouses* (1954). The book reflected contemporary deep-seated concerns about the rapid changes that were dramatically reshaping the British landscape, with its passionate text by Cook and Smith's visual paean to the humble delights of local building crafts and techniques that were sympathetic to locale and climate but increasingly threatened by insensitive redevelopment and the use of concrete (which Cook lambasted for being 'the most inexpressive of all materials, the most destructive of regional character'[7]). The spiritual importance and abundant variety of that landscape together with the country's built heritage were celebrated in two further Smith-illustrated Thames & Hudson publications, George Fraser's *Scotland* (1955) and Geoffrey Grigson's *England* (1957), which together breathed new life into the somewhat hidebound genre of topographical photography. More importantly, these books – sumptuously illustrated with photogravure reproductions that did full justice to the subtly nuanced tonality of Smith's original imagery – not only established Smith as a photographer of the first rank but also made a telling contribution to the post-war rediscovery of Britain and what constituted Britishness, concerns that were at the heart of the Neo-Romantic movement. Increasingly in the wake of their possible obliteration through bombing or untrammelled redevelopment, the country's landscape and buildings had come to define Britishness. This fragility encouraged artists such as John Piper, with whose work Smith's bears a spiritual kinship, to explore their native land with a new urgency and intensity. Significantly, Smith himself valued his 'negatives very much as a collection and as a record of places that are changing and disappearing'[8]. This is what gives them their strength – they are at once an inventory but also, with their carefully chosen subject-matter and controlled viewpoints, an inventive fabrication of an idyllic, unchanging world that is nevertheless threatened by dark forces beyond the frame, like W H Auden's cigarette end smouldering menacingly on the garden border.

13

Edwin Smith's work for Thames & Hudson obliged him to perfect a new photographic technique. The small format cameras he had employed before the war were unsuitable for architectural recording, which required larger cameras with a full range of movements, especially a rising front to counteract the problem of converging verticals. Smith thus purchased a second-hand, half-plate Ruby, a camera manufactured by Thornton Pickard of Leeds, together with a quarter-plate Sanderson and a smaller Ensign Autorange 820, which were more easily portable to subjects difficult to access. His compositional strategy also changed from one predominantly attuned to catching life on the fly to one that was much more carefully considered. In church interiors, for example, he revealed that he was 'drawn to situations where the source of light lies diagonally in front of me and not behind'[9] while, for exterior images, he preferred to photograph under a pallid sky rather than when the sun was at its most intense and consequently casting the deep shadows he was anxious to avoid. People now no longer appeared in his pictures as frequently as they had done in his pre-war work but as Betjeman remarked their traces were everywhere from the casually abandoned clutter of signage at the Booking Office, Talyllyn Railway, Merioneth, Wales (1959) [Plate 37] to the open milk bottle at Furlongs, Firle (1953) [Plate 6], the latter, though more comfortable, nevertheless reminiscent of Walker Evans's 1930s documentation of sharecropper's cabins in America's Depression-devastated Deep South.

The lyricism and tonal delicacy of Edwin Smith's imagery, together with his choice of primarily historical subject matter, placed him firmly in a photographic tradition that, though sustained by few practitioners, stretched back to the very roots of the medium. For its first two decades, the photography of buildings and landscape in Britain had been overwhelmingly in thrall to the doctrine of the Picturesque as articulated by theorists such as Uvedale Price. The influential commentator, Thomas Sutton, summed up the movement's stance when advising photographers in 1854 to ignore 'spick and span modern buildings' and concentrate on 'such grand scenes or artistic sites as a painter would select' to achieve 'the true poetry of photography'[10]. Smith's photograph of the romantically ruinous Bolton Priory (1959) [Plate 29], if printed on albumen paper, could easily be mistaken for a product of the 1850s, and would doubtless have earned Sutton's commendation with its typically picturesque musing on the transience of man's endeavours. By the 1860s, however, firms photographing contemporary architecture had come to dominate and it was not until the turn of the century, in the face of increasing industrialisation and the rise of Pictorialism, that the more picturesque approach to architectural recording enjoyed a revival as can be seen in the work of photographers such as Henry Bennett, Charles Latham in *Country Life*, and, above all, Frederick Evans (1853-1943). With his numinous renditions of cathedral interiors which were reckoned to have raised architectural photography from 'a matter of mere record into the domain of poetry and pictorial achievement'[11], Evans was Smith's spiritual forbear even though Smith's imagery was less mystical and more focussed on the earthbound.

The success of his books for Thames & Hudson saw Smith's work in greater demand than ever before during the last decade of his life with commissions from a wider range of publishers, among them Paul Elek and Weidenfeld and Nicolson, affording him the opportunity to explore buildings and landscapes further afield. The reproduction of some of his images in the prestigious postcard series published by Gordon Fraser also helped to broaden the popular audience for his work. While his technique remained unchanged, his subject matter revealed a newly discovered enchantment with gardens as witnessed especially by Edward Hyams's *The English Garden* (1964) and *English Cottage Gardens* (1970), as well as a deepening photographic engagement with landscape, the imagery of which caused Smith the most pride for in it he reckoned he 'had perhaps managed to convey something of infinity'[12]. This can perhaps be best seen in *Ireland*, published by Thames & Hudson in 1966 and written by the actor and theatre director Micheál Mac Liammóir, which prompted the Guardian's critic, W L Webb to enthuse,

> No prose coruscations can compete with the grave lyric beauty of Edwin Smith's photographs. This is not just the best landscape photography I have ever seen: it is so subtly responsive to the particular mysteries of light, image and perspective that the limits of the medium seem dissolved, and one passes from page to page through a series of frozen dreams.[13]

Although Smith travelled throughout Europe and produced a book on Athens as part of a series for Elek, the lyrical potency of his photography was most manifest in his Italian work. While his 1971 *Rome: From its Foundation to the Present* was a disappointment, the 1965 *The Wonders of Italy* was a masterpiece, with Smith's imagery lavishly and dramatically reproduced in Thames & Hudson's opulent publication. By contrast, *Pompeii and Herculaneum: the Glory and the Grief* (1960) was a much more modest work with Smith's photographs reproduced by Elek not in photogravure, but in the more prosaic half-tone which, as Smith later rightly complained, failed to do justice to the subtleties of his originals. Nevertheless it is a tribute to Smith's photography that despite this drawback the book proved an outstanding success. Indeed Smith's images of the towns destroyed by Vesuvius's eruption show the photographer at the very peak of his powers, demonstrating in the words of one reviewer 'a remarkable, almost sensuous feeling for surfaces and textures'[14]. They also represent a powerfully haunting elegy for a disappeared world. Two years later, Smith collaborated with the same author, Marcel Brion, on another Elek publication, *Venice: the Masque of Italy*, which revealed Smith revelling in the city's wealth of 'romantically pictorial experiences'[15]. Here he could give full expression to his delight in incongruity, tactile intensity, and 'knowing eye'[16], which allowed him to invest even the most seemingly mundane detail with special significance.

On the home front, Smith provided the imagery for new, updated books on *Scotland* (1968) and *England* (1971), but his most significant work was that for A J Youngson's seminal *The Making of Classical Edinburgh* (1966), which *House & Garden* lauded as 'one of the finest, most comprehensive and exploratory records of a city ever made'[17]. In images that alternated between the crisply detailed and languidly atmospheric, the latter exemplified by an elevated view of Edinburgh seen through a smoky haze, Smith created an exemplary visual complement to Youngson's text. Indeed it was photographs such as this that moved the critic Ken Powell to declare, 'For many of us, the late Edwin Smith's photographs ... were a gateway to the history of architecture'[18]. The importance of Smith's photography goes far beyond this, however. For most of his life Smith denied his calling as a photographer, wishing to establish himself as an artist instead and becoming bitterly disappointed at his failure to do so. Yet he could not hide his love of the medium, writing a series of primers about it, including *All the Photo-Tricks* (1940), going to the utmost lengths to achieve the perfect image, and confessing,

> The man who lives in his eyes is continually confronted with scenes and spectacles that compel his attention, or admiration, and demand an adequate reaction. To pass on without pause is impossible, and to continue after purely mental applause is unsatisfying, some real tribute must be paid. Photography, to many of its addicts, is a convenient and simple means of discharging these ever-recurring debts to the visual world.[19]

The humility of this statement encapsulates the essence of Smith's photography. It is not a photography of instant eye-catching drama that may initially arouse but subsequently disappoint, but of subtle intimation, gently beckoning and rewarding through prolonged contemplation. As his friend, the writer, Norman Scarfe, put it, Smith 'opened the eyes of a generation'[20]. He may be set to do so again.

Robert Elwall

1   For a more detailed account of Smith's photography, see Robert Elwall, *Evocations of Place: The Photography of Edwin Smith*, London: Merrell, 2007.

2   *Daily Telegraph* & *Morning Post*, 23 August 1954

3   *Modern Photography: the Studio Annual of Camera Art*, 1935-36, page 19

4   *The Saturday Book* 32, London: Hutchinson, 1972, page 6

5   John Betjeman, *Church Poems*, London: John Murray, 1981, page 7

6   Edwin Smith, 'On Photographing Cathedrals and Parish Churches', in Olive Cook, *English Parish Churches*, London: Thames & Hudson, 1976, page 7

7   Olive Cook, *English Cottages and Farmhouses*, London: Thames & Hudson, 1954, page 9

8   Letter from Smith to Trevor Thomas of Gordon Fraser, 28 April 1962 (Olive Cook Papers, Newnham College Archives, Cambridge, Box 34 6/3/7)

9   Edwin Smith, 'On Photographing Cathedrals and Parish Churches', op cit, page 6

10 *Journal of the Photographic Society*, vol 2, 21 October, pages 53-54

11 Quoted in Beaumont Newhall, *Frederick H. Evans*, Rochester, NY: George Eastman House, 1954, page 41

12 Quoted in Olive Cook, 'Edwin Smith – the Photographer', in *Record and Revelation: Photographs by Edwin Smith*, York: Impressions Gallery of Photography, 1983, [unpaginated]

13 *The Guardian*, 15 July 1966

14 *The Times Literary Supplement*, 29 March 1974, page 321

15 Letter from Smith to Cook, Venice, 20 September [1961] (Edwin Smith Collection, RIBA British Architectural Library Photographs Collection)

16 'Recollections by His Friends: Eva Neurath', in *Aspects of the Art of Edwin Smith*, 1974, [unpaginated]   17

17 *House & Garden*, March 1972, page 71

18 *Twentieth Century Society Newsletter*, Summer 2000, page 27

19 Edwin Smith, *All the Photo-Tricks*, London & New York: Focal Press, 1940, page 271

20 Quoted in Julia Hedgecoe, 'In Memoriam: Life Stories. Olive Muriel Smith', *Newnham College Roll Letter*, 2003, page 111

Edwin Smith & Olive Cook, 1958

'The man who lives in his eyes': The Aesthetic Orbit of Edwin Smith

The photographs of Edwin Smith achieve such an extraordinary sense of the spirit of a place that they can appear to exist almost independently of their creator. Yet, they are at once expressions of a highly developed personal taste and manifestations of preoccupations shared with many contemporary creative figures. So this essay seeks to sketch the genesis and hinterland of Smith's aesthetic.

1. Discharging a debt to the visual world

Edwin Smith once wrote that

> The man who lives in his eyes is continually confronted with scenes and spectacles that compel his attention or admiration and demand an adequate reaction. To pass on without pause is impossible and to continue after merely mental applause is unsatisfying: some real tribute must be paid[1].

He then added that 'Photography ... is a convenient and simple means of discharging this ever recurrent debt to the visual world.'

These words were included in *All the Photo-Tricks*, the most substantial of Smith's guides to photography, published in 1940, when Smith was twenty-eight. However, Norman Scarfe, an East Anglian writer with whom Smith collaborated, has suggested that they were written earlier still, when he was only twenty-five, and on the outset of an artistic career that was not certainly that of a photographer[2]. Thus they imply a more general approach to life and art, and a symbiosis between them.

Smith left school in 1924, at the age of twelve, to train as a builder and, four years later, as an architect, at the Northern Polytechnic, in Holloway, north London. However, he had, what he called, 'an incurable tendency very early in life of preferring the two-dimensional image to its three-dimensional counterpart'[3]. He also confessed to John Cecil Stephenson, Head of Art Teaching in the Architectural Department, that his ambition was to be a painter. And he did not necessarily deviate from that ambition when the work of Eugène Atget (1857-1927) awakened an interest in photography. Indeed, he justified his interest by identifying with this French photographer, who always considered himself a painter who happened to make photographic records.

And, perhaps, it is only right that he did identify with Atget, for both are now remembered principally as photographers, the work of whom was informed by – and is representative of – so much more. Both were memorialists of past and passing beauty, and enthusiasts for the more exuberant and potentially surreal elements of popular culture. Both may also be considered bulwarks against specifically *architectural* Modernism, Atget recording parts of Paris that were to be destroyed by the development of the Métro, Smith recoiling from the Puritanical character of much modern architecture, after the brief experience, in 1932, of working for the architect, Marshall Sisson.

2. A long and living tradition

If Edwin Smith's encounter with the work of Atget encouraged him to acquire his first camera (a Kodak Box Brownie) in about 1927, it was his friendship with the artist, Enid Marx (1902-1998), which led to the receipt of a second (a damaged quarter-plate camera) some seven years later. Though too few details are known about Smith's friendship with Marx, it is clear that she was supportive and *sympathique*, while her interests and the art works that resulted paralleled his.

Marx attended the Royal College of Art between 1922 and 1925, at the same time as Edward Bawden and Eric Ravilious and, like them, studied under the influential artist, Paul Nash. She then established herself as a designer and printer of textiles and papers, as well as a painter, in St John's Wood. A collector from an early age, she developed a particular interest and expertise in various popular arts, and drew inspiration from the indigenous tradition. She also wrote studies of popular art in collaboration with her friend, the historian, Margaret Lambert[4].

Robert Elwall has noticed a particular analogy between Marx and Lambert's illustrated scrapbook, *When Victoria Began to Reign*, published in 1937, and Smith's 'documentation of that year's popular festivities marking the coronation of King George VI'[5]. More generally, they were drawn to the same phenomena of 'a long and living tradition of popular art'[6], including fairs and circuses, and also Victorian toy theatres. Marx must have spurred Smith on in his comprehensive project to photograph fairs and circuses, in the years 1935-38 [Plate 1], and may have joined him in his visits to Pollock's Toy Theatre shop, in Hoxton, as she did Eric Ravilious. (Smith would work with Benjamin Pollock Ltd after the Second World War, and his collection of toy theatre material entered Pollock's

Toy Museum in 2002.) She certainly encouraged him to persevere with making wood- and linocuts, which he began in 1933, and which perhaps comprise the best of his visual work outside photography.

Marx and Smith were not alone in championing popular and traditional art, but rather part of a loose confederacy that gathered strength between the wars and proved a force in the post-war era. So when Smith's second wife, Olive Cook, visited the Festival of Britain, on London's South Bank, in 1951, she encountered installations that exuded 'humour and fantasy of a kind' that she had always thought 'peculiar' to Smith[7]. These included decorations by Edward Bawden, Kenneth Rowntree and others for the Lion and Unicorn Pavilion, which was described by one visitor as:

> an unashamed celebration of 'Englishness' as it was then perceived to be. There was a touch of humour here, of a gentle Punch like variety and more than a few hints of Popular Folk Art, coupled with an inclination toward Victoriana[8]

At the same time, across the river, the Whitechapel Art Gallery held 'Black Eyes and Lemonade', an exhibition of popular art, curated and designed by Barbara Jones (1912-1978). Jones included at least two photographs by Smith in *The Unsophisticated Arts*, the book that was published to accompany the exhibition. These are of Chinese flowers or shivery-shakes, 'elaborately fretted concertinas of bright paper' sold at fairs[9].

Jones, Marx, Smith and Cook have been linked together as a 'sub-group' of enthusiasts, who

> particularly favoured Louis Meier's antique shop in Cecil Court and the second-hand booksellers of Farringdon Road, but the pursuit of the vernacular was competitive; if one of the group saw something piquant in a junk-shop 'you couldn't tell Barbara [Jones] or she'd be there ahead of you'[10]

With regards to Smith and Cook, this 'pursuit of the vernacular' would manifest itself with particular distinction in the eclectically illustrated contributions that they wrote and designed for the wide-ranging annual miscellany, *The Saturday Book*, from 1944 (number 4) to 1975 (the last, number 34, which appeared four years after Smith's death).

3. Neo-Romanticism

Enid Marx also helped launch Edwin Smith's photographic career by introducing him and his work to her former teacher, Paul Nash. Having taken up photography in about 1930 as an adjunct to his painting, Nash responded very positively to Smith's images, and perhaps recognised his own influence in them. As a result, he 'arranged for him to use the darkroom of the publisher Lund Humphries outside normal office hours, thus freeing Smith from reliance on local chemists to process his film'[11]. In addition, he introduced Smith to the editor of British *Vogue*, so facilitating his first contributions to publications, in 1935.

Within two years, in 1937, Smith was receiving regular commissions through Marcus Brumwell, the Managing Director of the Stuart Advertising Agency. He may have met other artists on the agency's books at this time, including Edward Bawden, another of Nash's former students, and John Piper, one of Nash's friends.

Piper's career resonated with that of Smith for, in valuing and recording the native heritage, they, like Nash, rehearsed the Romantic tradition, and would be considered as 'Neo-Romantics'[12], a term coined by Robin Ironside in the late 1930s[13]. It was in 1937 that Piper was introduced to John Betjeman, who was editor of the Shell Guides, and a year later, published *Oxon*, initiating his own significant contribution to the series. In the post-war period, Smith would contribute photographs to Norman Scarfe's Shell Guide to Suffolk (1960) and other of the volumes. However, Scarfe has recounted that Piper would have preferred to have excluded Smith's photographs, precisely – if perversely – because

> Edwin had this feeling that he wasn't so much a photographer as a painter and John Piper's feeling was I think to some extent that he was a great photographer and not a great painter.[14]

Fortunately, Smith was not reliant on the Shell Guides in order to publish his photographs, and thus to communicate his sensibilities. He would parallel, and widen, the focus of the Shell Guides in his work for Thames & Hudson and other publishers, sometimes in collaboration with Olive Cook.

4. Olive Cook

Edwin Smith's meeting with Olive Cook, in 1943, on the stairs of the Hampstead building in which they both lived, was arguably the most significant event in his life. While they shared a very similar taste and outlook, Cook's more academic background and analytical bent complemented his auto-didacticism and instinctive eye, and so made her an ideal partner in work; while her warmth, generosity and talent for friendship gave him security and happiness at home. Furthermore, her experiences did much to enrich his growing artistic circle.

Having graduated from Cambridge with a degree in French and German, in 1934, Cook moved to London, and worked first for the publishers, Chatto & Windus, and then, from 1937, as supervisor of publications at the National Gallery. Through its enterprising and well-connected Director, Kenneth Clark, she met a number of contemporary artists, including Paul Nash. Indeed, in the years before they met, she and Smith must have had a number of acquaintances, if not friends, in common.

One of Cook's closest friends during this period was the painter and writer, Thomas Hennell. Their initial encounter was not auspicious for, while working for Chatto, she rejected his 'manuscript of a lengthy illustrated poem'. However, 'the friendship developed after Tom chanced to meet Olive in the National Gallery'[15]. As a result, she stayed with him on several occasions at his home, at Orchard Cottage, Ridley, Kent, and while there met other artists, such as Graham Sutherland. Like Smith, Cook had ambitions to be a painter, and she may have received lessons from Hennell. It has also been said that he once proposed to her; certainly they remained close until his disappearance in Indonesia in 1945, while working as an Official War Artist.

Cook had more success than Smith as a painter, though her formal training seems to have been confined to a short course taken at Cedric Morris's East Anglian School of Painting and Drawing in, or around, 1940. In 1941, she was invited to participate in the ambitious Recording Britain scheme, possibly at the suggestion of Kenneth Clark, who had devised it. Funded by the American organisation, the Pilgrim Trust, this scheme was established in 1939 to record, and preserve on paper, the natural and man-made environments of Britain that were threatened both externally by military invasion and internally by industrial and social change. Of the many artists who worked for the scheme, the most relevant to Cook and Smith were Barbara Jones, Enid Marx, Thomas Hennell and John Piper – and also Michael Rothenstein and Kenneth Rowntree, who may have become friends at this time. Artists were allotted different regions and, on the evidence of two watercolours in the Victoria & Albert Museum, Cook spent some time in west Cornwall and was in North Wales in September 1943. (When at home in London, she continued to work at the National Gallery and served as an air raid warden.)

When Cook met Smith in 1943, he was married, to Rosemary Ansell, and had recently become the father of a son, Martin. The war for him seems to have been an uncomfortable and uncertain time, as is only emphasised by the lack of documentary evidence. Soon after the outbreak of war, in 1939, he was called-up to serve in the forces and, on failing to respond to this, had to attend a tribunal to explain his behaviour. It has been said that, objecting to war on principle, he walked out and spent time on the run, but also that he worked for a while as a camouflage artist[16]. Cook proved an anchor.

5. Among Exiles

Despite his difficulties, Edwin Smith still tried to develop as a draughtsman and painter, as is indicated by a number of surviving sketchbooks for the years 1939 to 1944[17]. He would have been encouraged in these activities not only by Olive Cook, but also by two émigré artists whom he befriended: Oskar Kokoschka (1886-1980), from Austria, and Zdzislaw Ruszkowski (1907-1991), from Poland.

Identified as a degenerate artist by the Nazis, Kokoschka fled to Britain in 1938, and spent much of the war in London. Having met him by 1943, Smith joined Kokoschka and his wife, Olda, on a painting trip to Nevin, Caernarvonshire, North Wales, in the April of that year. And, given that Cook and the Kokoschkas were both painting in North Wales in the September, it is possible that they were together, and in the company of Smith. Cook's watercolour, *Backyard of the Abbey Arms Hotel, Festiniog, N Wales* (V&A), may even record one of the places at which they stayed. Cook had known of the area since 1940, when she helped supervise the removal of paintings from the National Gallery, in London, to slate mines between Blaenau Festiniog and Festiniog, in order to protect them from German air raids.

Back in London, late in 1943, Smith and Kokoschka spent a good deal of time together, as is indicated by several visits that they made to the Bedford Theatre, Camden Town, in the December. Smith was undoubtedly drawn by the

Bedford's reputation as a music hall, Kokoschka possibly because it had been painted by Walter Sickert.

Then, in the summer of 1944, Kokoschka provided a preface for the catalogue to 'Cats and Women', the only show of Smith's artwork to be held in his lifetime, at the Berkeley Galleries, Davies Street. Ruszkowski was equally supportive, and would recollect that 'all Edwin's creations were done with perfect knowledge of materials and technique and with precision of execution'[18]. Neverthless, Smith sold just one work of the eighty paintings, drawings and prints, and later stated drily that he was 'the only artist with a complete collection of his own work'[19].

While Smith and Cook achieved more in other fields of creativity as, respectively, photographer and writer, the neglect of their work as painters may be due more to the difficulty of situating it in time and place, and less to their lack of talent. Stylistically, their painted images may have more in common with European Expressionism, and may have been influenced by the likes of Kokoschka and Ruszkowski. However, in interests and attitudes they fitted neatly into the indigenous artistic communities that centred on Furlongs and Great Bardfield.

6. Furlongs, Great Bardfield … and Saffron Walden

In 1947, Edwin Smith and Olive Cook made the first of many visits to Furlongs, an isolated farmstead, near Firle, East Sussex [Plates 5 & 6]. Since 1933, this had been the country retreat of Peggy Angus (1904-1993), the innovative designer and painter, who had studied at the Royal College of Art alongside Edward Bawden, Helen Binyon, Enid Marx and Eric Ravilious. Initially, she rented one of two Victorian flint shepherd's cottages, and gradually transformed it into 'a showpiece of decorative achievement'[20]. She shared the experience with her husband, James Maude Richards, the editor of *The Architectural Review*, following their marriage in 1936, but also with a stream of artist friends. As accommodation was limited and basic, guests stayed in two Boer fever wagons, which had been discovered and acquired by Ravilious and his artist wife, Tirzah, in 1934. In the years before the Second World War, Ravilious was one of the most regular visitors, often staying with Binyon, who became his lover. However, Bawden and his wife, Charlotte, stayed only once, ostensibly because he found it too uncomfortable.

By the time that Smith and Cook arrived, circumstances had changed. Angus and Richards had drifted apart, and would divorce in 1948. Ravilious, like his friend Hennell, had disappeared presumed dead while serving as an Official War Artist. Guests were now accommodated in the second cottage. Yet, the daily round went on as before, with friends expected to busy themselves in artistic activity. In writing an obituary of Angus, Cook remembered fondly 'the feeling of closeness to nature, the cosiness and colour of firelight and lamplight in the rich little rooms, the stimulating conversations and the conviviality of the evenings'[21]. On some of those evenings, Cook and Smith performed magic lantern shows and toy theatre plays while, at Midsummer and on Guy Fawkes Night, Angus held parties. 'The matrix of much strange and inventive creation' was how Angus herself described Furlongs[22].

The village of Great Bardfield, in north-west Essex, was also a creative matrix, but one on a larger scale and of greater permanence. Olive Cook and Edwin Smith were drawn to East Anglia in general, and Great Bardfield in particular, for various reasons. Cook was herself an East Anglian, having been born, brought up and educated in Cambridge, and her first guidebook was on Suffolk (1948). She and Smith found in Great Bardfield a ready-made circle, and one that upheld the values they held dear. Like them, Great Bardfield artists tended to be nourished by vernacular, popular tradition, and were keen to maintain and record Britain in the rich variety of its environment and way of life.

At the centre of the circle was Brick House, 'a three-storey Georgian building on the High Street with an acre of garden behind it'[23]. Bawden and Ravilious rented half of it as a weekend retreat from 1925, and they met Hennell there, in 1931, when he was lodging in the other half. Then, when Bawden married Charlotte Epton, the painter and potter, in 1932, his father bought the whole house and gave it to them as a wedding present. For the first two years of their marriage, the Bawdens shared it with the Raviliouses, until they moved to Castle Hedingham, ten miles away. In 1933, John Aldridge and his wife, Lucie, moved into the village, buying the Elizabethan Place House and, to a degree, stepping into the Raviliouses' shoes. Not only did Edward and John share a love of gardening; they also collaborated on making hand-blocked wallpapers just before the war.

During the war, the Bawdens and John Aldridge worked away from Great Bardfield, but new arrivals ensured that artistic activity continued. Notable among these were Ravilious' former student, Kenneth Rowntree, and his wife, the architect, Diana Buckley (who stayed in the village until 1949), and Michael Rothenstein and his wife, the painter, Duffy Ayres (who stayed until 1953). After the war, they were joined by Bawden's former students – Bernard Cheese and his wife, Sheila Robinson, and Walter Hoyle – among others.

Though Cook and Smith did not move to the village, they often visited for weekends, staying with the Bawdens or the Aldridges, and taking an enthusiastic part in their fancy dress parties and charades. Cook developed a particular friendship with Duffy Ayres, as she did with Ravilious' widow, Tirzah. (Following her second marriage in 1946, to BBC producer, Henry Swanzy, Tirzah lived in Hampstead, and together they brought up James, her son by Ravilious. During Tirzah's final illness, leading to her death in 1951, Cook looked after James and became 'almost a godmother' to him[24]. James grew up to become a photographer of the English landscape, and as such may be considered an heir to Edwin Smith. Indeed, Cook gave him one of Smith's cameras.)

In 1962, Cook and Smith settled in Saffron Walden, to the north-west of Great Bardfield, so strengthening their alliance to the area and its artists. They were active in the local arts festival, and campaigned to protect nearby Stansted from the development of a third London airport (publishing *The Stansted Affair* in 1967). They lived first at 3 Audley Road and, from 1967, at the Coach House, Windmill Hill, both of which they 'remodelled and decorated ... in the romantic image of an earlier time'[25]. It was an approach to interior design that they shared with Bawden, and also Bawden's friend, Betty Swanwick, whose memorable toy theatre productions at Goldsmiths' College they had attended (in the period 1943-64). When Bawden's wife died in 1970, he moved to Saffron Walden to be closer to friends, including Cook, who was herself soon widowed, Smith dying in 1971.

In later years, Cook did much to promote her husband's work, but also that of the artists of north-west Essex. She wrote retrospective articles and catalogues, and was instrumental in the foundation of the Fry Art Gallery, Saffron Walden, which opened in 1987, and of which Bawden became a patron and donor (before his death in 1989). As late as the years 1998-99, she revived the spirit of Great Bardfield in collaborations with Walter Hoyle for the Previous Parrot Press: writing the story, *Tryphema Pruss: The Ghost of a Great Lodge*, for him to illustrate, and providing an introduction to his account, *To Sicily with*

Edward Bawden. The latter appeared with illustrations by Edwin Smith, as well as by Hoyle and Bawden. By so doing, it acted as a reminiscence of Cook and Smith's own travels in Sicily and Italy, and also a reminder that – even as a photographer – Smith was, at one level, essentially an illustrator.

Since the death of Cook in 2002, the Fry Art Gallery has gone from strength to strength, with the artists of north-west Essex continuing to gain in popularity. A visitor to its charming rooms will now discover photographs by Edwin Smith hanging in the entrance, photographs that are immediately recognisable and individual and yet that, at the same time, sit so happily in the context of other exponents of a strong and distinctive strand of British art.

Smith will rightly be remembered as a photographer, but his photographs will be remembered because of all that informs them: a range of artistic practices, a breadth of taste, an attentive eye, a developed sense of humanity, and the traces of like-minded friends.

David Wootton

1   Edwin Smith, *All the Photo-Tricks*, London & New York: Focal Press, 1940, page 271
2   Norman Scarfe, *Edwin Smith 1912-1971. Photographs, Paintings & Drawings*, House, 62 Regents Park Road, London NW1, November-December 1976, [unpaginated]
3   Edwin Smith, *Modern Photography: The Studio Annual of Camera Art*, 1935-36, page 19
4   The Marx-Lambert collection was bequeathed by Enid Marx to Compton Verney, Warwickshire, in 1998.
5   Robert Elwall, *Evocations of Place: The Photography of Edwin Smith*, London: Merrell, 2007, page 17
6   Enid Marx and Margaret Lambert, *English Popular and Traditional Art*, London: Collins, 1946, page 7
7   Letter from Cook to Smith, quoted in Robert Elwall, op cit, page 26
8   Ian Mackenzie-Kerr, quoted on the Museum of London's website, www.museumoflondon.org.uk. A book designer for Thames & Hudson from 1957, Mackenzie-Kerr developed a strong friendship with Cook and Smith through working on their books.
9   Barbara Jones, *The Unsophisticated Arts*, London: The Architectural Press, 1951, page 140

10 David Mellor, '"Recording Britain": A History and Outline', in David Mellor, Gill Saunders and Patrick Wright, *Recording Britain. A Pictorial Domesday of Pre-War Britain*, Newton Abbot: David & Charles in association with the Victoria and Albert Museum, 1990, page 18, quoting an interview with Olice Cook

11 Elwall, op cit, page 13

12 The work of Edwin Smith was, for instance, well represented in the exhibition, 'A Paradise Lost. The Neo-Romantic Imagination in Britain 1935-55', held at the Barbican Art Gallery in 1987.

13 See Malcolm Yorke, *The Spirit of Place. Nine Neo-Romantic Artists and Their Times*, London: Taurus Parke, 2001, page 23

14 Quoted by Brian Human in 'Capturing Paradise: Edwin Smith Painting & Drawing', published on the website, www.weepingash.co.uk

15 Michael MacLeod, *Thomas Hennell. Countryman, artist and writer*, Cambridge University Press, page 69

16 See Brian Human, 'Edwin Smith: Unwrapping the Enigma', published on the website, www.weepingash.co.uk

17 See Brian Human, 'Capturing Paradise: Edwin Smith Painting & Drawing', published on the website, www.weepingash.co.uk

18 Included in *Aspects of the Art of Edwin Smith*, Colchester: The Minories, 1974, [unpaginated]

19 Quoted by Olive Cook and Roy Hammans in 'Paintings & Drawings by Edwin Smith', published on the website, www.weepingash.co.uk

20 Obituary, *The Times*, 3 November 1993, page 21

21 Obituary, *Guardian*, 2 November 1993

22 *Furlongs. Peggy and Angus and Friends*, Eastbourne: Towner Art Gallery, 1987, [unpaginated]

23 Malcolm Yorke, 'Great Bardfield' in Martin Salisbury (ed), *Artists at the Fry. Art and Design in The North West Essex Collection*, Cambridge: Ruskin Press in association with the Fry Art Gallery, 2003, page 20

24 Peter Hamilton, *An English Eye. The Photographs of James Ravilious*, Tiverton: Devon Books, 1998, page 16

25 Brian Human, 'Olive Cook – A Brief Biography', published on the website, www.weepingash.co.uk

British Isles

With the exception of plate 43, which was printed in the early 1970s, all prints are hand-printed on 20 x 24 inch, silver gelatin paper, in 2010, from the original negatives.

Each of these is stamped with the ink-stamp of the RIBA British Architectural Library Photographs Collection, inscribed with title, numbered, and authenticated by Chris Beetles on reverse.

1. Mitcham Fair, London, 1935

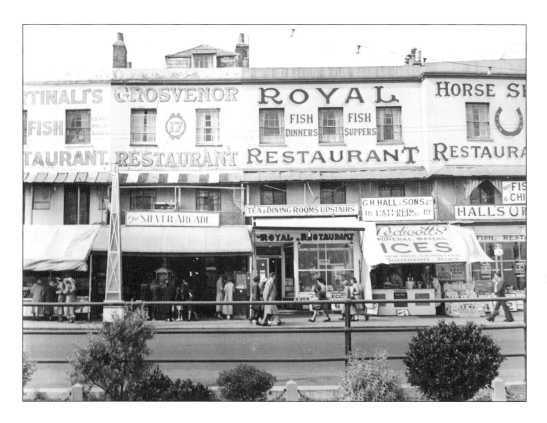

2. Seafront, Southend-on-Sea, Essex, 1940s

3. Brighton Beach, East Sussex, 1952

Illustrated: Geoffrey Grigson, *England*, London: Thames & Hudson, 1957, plate 28

Literature: Robert Elwall, *Evocations of Place: The Photography of Edwin Smith*, London: Merrell, 2007, page 87

35

4. The Beach, Eastbourne, East Sussex, 1955

Literature: Robert Elwall, *Evocations of Place: The Photography of Edwin Smith*, London: Merrell, 2007, page 99

5. Peggy Angus's House, Furlongs, Near Firle, East Sussex, 1961

6. The Kitchen of Peggy Angus's House, Furlongs, Near Firle,
   East Sussex, 1953

Literature: Robert Elwall, *Evocations of Place: The Photography
                of Edwin Smith*, London: Merrell, 2007, page 62

7. Thatching at Puddingcake Farm, Near Tenderden, Kent, 1953

8. Canterbury Cathedral, Kent, 1955
   Crypt

9. The Royal Exchange, Cornhill, London, 1957

Illustrated: Raymond Smith, *The Living City: A New View of the City of London*, London: Thames & Hudson, 1957, plate 45

Literature: Robert Elwall, *Evocations of Place: The Photography of Edwin Smith*, London: Merrell, 2007, page 80

10. The Royal Courts of Justice, Strand, London, 1970
    Seen from the south-east

11. Temple Bar, Theobalds Park, Cheshunt, Hertfordshire, 1968

12. Queen's House, Greenwich, London, 1970
    The Tulip Staircase

44

13. Woburn Abbey, Bedfordshire, 1961
    The Sculpture Gallery

14. Hardwick House, Bury St Edmunds, Suffolk, 1955
    Wrought iron gateway

Literature: Robert Elwall, *Evocations of Place: The Photography of*
                Edwin Smith, London: Merrell, 2007, page 89

15. Ely Cathedral, Cambridgeshire, 1958
    The west tower and southwest transept with two turret towers

16. The Triangular Bridge, Crowland, Lincolnshire, 1958

Illustrated: Angus Wilson and Olive Cook, *England*, London:
                 Thames & Hudson, 1971, plate 34
Literature: Robert Elwall, *Evocations of Place: The Photography of
                 Edwin Smith*, London: Merrell, 2007, page 105

17. Limetree Cottage, East Hagbourne, Berkshire, 1953

Illustrated: Olive Cook, *English Cottages and Farmhouses*,
                 London: Thames & Hudson, 1954, Plate 1
Literature: Robert Elwall, *Evocations of Place: The Photography of
                 Edwin Smith*, London: Merrell, 2007, page 53

18. Tithe Barn, Great Coxwell, Berkshire, 1953

Illustrated: Angus Wilson and Olive Cook, *England*, London:
Thames & Hudson, 1971, plate 46

Literature: Robert Elwall, *Evocations of Place: The Photography of
Edwin Smith*, London: Merrell, 2007, page 72

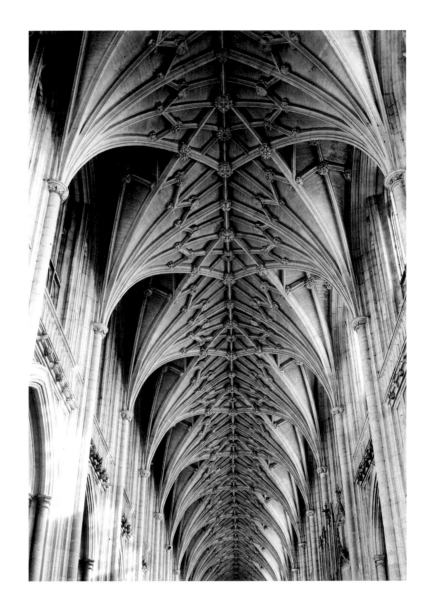

19. Winchester Cathedral, Hampshire, 1959
   The nave vault

20. Salisbury Cathedral, Wiltshire, 1959
   The west front

21. St Lawrence, Didmarton, Gloucestershire, 1961
   The vestry, formerly the north transept

Literature: Robert Elwall, *Evocations of Place: The Photography of
                Edwin Smith, London: Merrell, 2007, page 131

22. Daneway House, Sapperton, Gloucestershire, 1960
   View of the hall from the library

23. Newly Ploughed Field, Holkham, Norfolk, 1970

Literature: Robert Elwall, *Evocations of Place: The Photography of Edwin Smith*, London: Merrell, 2007, page 170

24. Football Match, Avebury, Wiltshire, 1962

25. Wells Cathedral, Somerset, 1968
   Stairs to the Chapter House

26. Wells Cathedral, Somerset, 1968
   The strainer arch seen from the south transept

27. Roofscape, Whitby, North Yorkshire, 1959

Literature: Robert Elwall, *Evocations of Place: The Photography of Edwin Smith*, London: Merrell, 2007, frontispiece

28. Whitby Abbey, North Yorkshire, 1954

29. Bolton Priory, North Yorkshire, 1959
   The ruined transepts

Illustrated: Olive Cook, *English Abbeys and Priories*,
                London: Thames & Hudson, 1960, plate 28

30. Fountains Abbey, North Yorkshire, 1959
    The Cellarium beneath the Brethen's Dorter

31. York Minster, 1958
   The nave looking east

32. York Minster, 1960
   The south transept seen from a side street

33. St Mary the Virgin, Pembridge, Herefordshire, 1961

34. Hadrian's Wall, Northumberland, 1959
   Looking east from Hotbank Crags

Illustrated: Angus Wilson and Olive Cook, *England*, London:
                 Thames & Hudson, 1971, plate 46

35. Edinburgh, looking west from The Crags to the Castle, 1954

Literature: Robert Elwall, *Evocations of Place: The Photography of
               Edwin Smith*, London: Merrell, 2007, page 75

36. The National Gallery of Scotland and The Mound seen from East Princes Street
   Gardens, Edinburgh, 1964

37. Booking Office, Talyllyn Railway, Merioneth, Wales, 1959

38. St Brigid's Well, Liscannor, County Clare, Ireland, 1965

Literature: Robert Elwall, *Evocations of Place: The Photography of
                Edwin Smith*, London: Merrell, 2007, page 154

39. Homestead, Ballinaboy, County Galway, Ireland, 1965

Illustrated: Olive Cook, *The English House through Seven Centuries*,
London: Nelson, 1968, page 11

40. Turf-cutting near Leenane, County Galway, Ireland, 1965

Illustrated: Micheál Mac Liammóir and Olive Cook, *Ireland*,
                London: Thames & Hudson, 1966, plate 75

41. St Ives, Cornwall, 1964

Italy

42. Fragments of the Colossal Statue of Constantine the Great, Palazzo dei
Conservatori, Rome, 1954

43. The Vatican Gardens, Rome, 1962

Stamped with photographer's ink stamp and inscribed with title on reverse
silver gelatin print, mounted on board, printed early 1970s
14 3/4 x 19 1/2 inches
Exhibited: 'Edwin Smith (1912-1971). A memorial exhibition of his photographs',
           Aldeburgh Festival, June-July 1973, no 59

44. St Peter's Basilica seen from the bastions of Castel Sant'Angelo, Rome, 1957

45. Fontana dell'Organo and Fonta di Nettuno, Villa d'Este, Tivoli, Lazio, 1960

46. Basilica of San Marco, Venice, 1961

Literature: Olive Cook, *The Wonders of Italy*, London: Thames & Hudson, 1965, plate 55

47. Piazza San Marco, Venice, 1961

48. Santa Maria della Salute and the Dogana de Mare seen from the flooded
Molo during 'Acqua Alta', Venice, 1961

49. Market from the Rialto Bridge, Venice, 1961

50. Palazzo Borromeo, Isola Bella, Lago Maggiore, 1960

51. The Lagoon, Venice, 1961

Literature: Robert Elwall, *Evocations of Place: The Photography of Edwin Smith*, London: Merrell, 2007, page 135

52. Camaldoni, Tuscany, 1963

53. Villa Garzoni, Collodi, Tuscany, 1962

Illustrated: Olive Cook, *The Wonders of Italy*, London: Thames & Hudson, 1965, Plate 55

Literature: Robert Elwall, *Evocations of Place: The Photography of Edwin Smith*, London: Merrell, 2007, page 145

54. A house on the edge of the village of Irsina, Basilicata, 1963

55. Farmhouse between Auletta and Potenza, Basilicata, 1963

Literature: Robert Elwall, *Evocations of Place: The Photography of Edwin Smith*, London: Merrell, 2007, page 143

56. The Great Palaestra, Pompeii, Campania, 1959

Edwin Smith and Olive Cook: A Chronology

1: Separate Lives

| 1912: | 20 February: Olive Muriel Cook [OC] was born at The Maisonette, 43 Garden Walk, Chesterton, Cambridge, the daughter of Arthur Hugh Cook, a librarian at Cambridge University Library, and his wife Kate, née Webb, a dressmaker for Robert Sayle, the local department store. |

15 May: Edwin George Herbert Smith [ES] was born at 2 St Paul's Road, Camden Town, London, the only child of Edwin Stanley Smith and his wife, Lily Beatrice, née Gray.

1914-18: ES and his mother lived with his aunt and grandmother at Ponder's End.

ES spent his childhood and adolescence with his mother in two rooms in St Pancras Way.

ES was educated at the LCC elementary school, Great College Street, Camden Town.

OC won a scholarship to the Perse School for Girls, Cambridge.

1922-23: OC and her family moved to 8 Leys Road.

1924: ES left school to attend the Northern Polytechnic, Holloway, to study a range of practical building crafts.

Circa 1927: ES encountered reproductions of the work of Eugène Atget. This led him to acquire his first camera, a Kodak Box Brownie, by redeeming cornflake-packet coupons.

1928: ES transferred to the Architectural Department of the Northern Polytechnic, as the result of a scholarship. One of his teachers, John Cecil Stephenson, encouraged him in his ambition to become a painter.

1929: OC was awarded a Certificate au Grand Concours Special by the Société Nationale de Professeurs de Français en Angleterre.

By 1930: ES was playing violin in the orchestra of the Northern Polytechnic.

1930: ES won a place at the Architectural Association.

1931: OC won a scholarship to Newnham College, Cambridge University, and took the Modern and Mediaeval Tripos (French and German). She would visit Germany several times.

1932: ES was forced to give up his place on the course at the Architectural Association before he had qualified. This was a result of his mother's straightened circumstances, his father having left some time before. With the help of the architect, James Burford, he gained a position as an architectural draughtsman in the office of Marshall Sisson, designer of Modernist houses.

ES worked as an architectural draughtsman for the Modernist architect, Raymond Myerscough-Walker.

1933: ES began to make wood-engravings and lino cuts.

1934: OC was awarded a 2.2 by Cambridge University.

OC moved to London, lodging in Hampstead and working as a typographer with Chatto & Windus, publishers.

Circa 1934: ES was given a damaged quarter-plate camera by his friend, Enid Marx. She introduced ES to her former teacher, Paul Nash, at a party. Nash then arranged for ES to use the darkroom of the publisher, Lund Humphries, outside normal office hours – and introduced him to the editor of the British edition of *Vogue*.

1935: Photographs by ES appeared in *Vogue*.

7 September: ES married Rosemary Ansell, a confectioner's daughter from Mitcham, Surrey. Initially, they lived with ES's mother.

ES would mainly use a refined version of the Contax, a 35 mm camera, originally introduced by Zeiss Ikon in 1932. He turned increasingly to photography as a means of support, and taking a wide range of subjects.

1935-38: ES made a comprehensive photographic version of fairground and circus.

1936: Summer: ES visited and photographed Newcastle, South Shields, Gateshead and the colliery at Ashington, at the behest of Sir Arnold Talbot Wilson, National Conservative MP for Hitchin.

Mid 1930s: Visited Germany, Belgium and Czechoslovakia.

Circa 1936: OC became supervisor of publications at the National Gallery and, through the Director, Kenneth Clark, met a number of contemporary artists.

ES was regularly commissioned by Marcus Brumwell's Stuart Advertising Agency.

Circa 1937: OC developed a close friendship with the artist and writer, Thomas Hennell, and would stay at his home at Orchard Cottage, Ridley, Kent, on several occasions.

1938: ES collaborated with Oswell Blakeston on *Phototips on Cats and Dogs: Not for Beginners Only* (the first of six books for Focal Press).

1939: ES attended a tribunal to explain why he had not answered the call-up to serve in the forces. He walked out and spent much of the Second World War on the run. However, he may also have worked for a year or two as a camouflage artist.

1940:	ES published *All the Photo-Tricks* (Focal Press).
	ES and his first wife, Rosemary, moved to the top floor flat, 38 Rosslyn Hill, Hampstead.
	OC became an air raid warden in Hampstead (until 1945).
Circa 1940:	OC spent two weeks studying art under Cedric Morris at the East Anglian School of Painting and Drawing, Benton End, Hadleigh.
1940-41:	She worked closely with him on the removal of the gallery's work to slate mines at Manod, between Blaenau Festiniog and Festiniog.
1941:	ES's son, Martin, was born.
	OC was invited to participate in the Recording Britain Scheme. Works included *Backyard of the Abbey Arms Hotel, Festiniog, N Wales* (September 1943) and *Disused Tin Mine, St Agnes, Cornwall* (no date) (both in the V&A).

2: Together in London

1943:	ES abandoned his wife and son for OC, who was also living in a flat at 38 Rosslyn Hill.
	January: Rayner Heppenstall published *Saturnine* (Secker & Warburg), an autobiographical novel, the characters of which include the photographer, Aloysius Smith, based on ES.
	April: ES travelled to Nevin, Caernarvonshire, North Wales, with Oskar and Olda Kokoschka.
	December: ES made several visits to performances at the Bedford Theatre, Camden Town, in the company of Kokoschka.
1944:	Summer: ES held the only show of his artwork in his lifetime. 'Cats and Women' was held at the Berkeley Galleries, Davies Street, London, and was accompanied by a catalogue with a preface by Kokoschka. Of the 80 oils, watercolours, drawings and prints, only 1 sold.
	ES became the first British friend of the Polish émigré artist, Zdzislaw Ruszkowski.
	ES and OC contributed to *The Saturday Book* for the first time.
1945:	OC left the National Gallery to pursue a freelance career in painting and writing.
Mid 1940s:	ES acquired an Ensign Autorange 820 camera, which has a Ross Xpres lens.
1946:	ES's first marriage was dissolved.
	ES illustrated W S Scott's *A Clowder of Cats* (John Westhouse).

1947:	ES and OC made the first of many visits to Furlongs, the isolated farmstead, near Firle, East Sussex, rented by the painter and designer, Peggy Angus.
1948:	OC produced the first of her guide books, *Suffolk* (Elek, in the Visions of England series), illustrated by Rowland Suddaby, with some photographs by ES.
	March: OC lectured on 'The Painting of English Landscape' at Jesus College, Cambridge.
1950:	ES and OC made their first visit to Sicily, to participate in a painting competition in Agrigento. OC won the second prize, the money enabling them to stay for several months.
Circa 1950:	OC often looked after James Ravilious, the son of Eric and Tirza, during his mother's illness, and remained a close friend after her death in 1951.
1951:	ES contributed photographs to Barbara Jones' *The Unsophisticated Arts* (Architectural Press).
	ES edited Ralph Mayer's *The Artist's Handbook of Material and Techniques* for its publication in Britain by Faber & Faber.
1952:	ES collaborated with Graham Hutton on *English Parish Churches*, his first book of architectural photographs, and his first for Thames & Hudson. For this project, and subsequently, he used a 1904 Ruby half-plate field camera, by Thornton Pickard, and a quarter-plate Sanderson camera.
	OC became the English representative for the Carnegie Institute at Pittsburgh (until 1964).
1954:	ES and OC were living at 29 Buckland Crescent, Hampstead.
	7 September: ES married OC.
	ES and OC returned to Sicily.
	ES and OC collaborated together for the first time for Thames & Hudson, on *English Cottages and Farmhouses*.
	OC produced her first work of fiction: children's stories for *House* (Thames & Hudson, in the Playbook Library series), with nursery friezes by George Adams. ES edited the revised edition of Hilaire Hiler's *Notes on the Technique of Painting* (Faber & Faber).
1955:	ES collaborated with George Fraser on *Scotland* (Thames & Hudson).
1956:	ES and OC collaborated on *Breckland* (Robert Hale).
	OC was a visiting tutor in painting and architecture at the WI's Denman College, Abingdon, Oxfordshire.

1957:   ES collaborated with Geoffrey Grigson on *England* (Thames & Hudson).

1960:   ES and OC collaborated on *English Abbeys and Priories* (Thames & Hudson).

ES collaborated with Marcel Brion on *Pompeii and Herculaneum: The Glory and the Grief* (Elek Books).

1961:   ES collaborated with Sacheverell Sitwell on *Great Houses of Europe* (Weidenfeld & Nicolson).

3: Saffron Walden

1962:   ES and OC moved to 3 Audley Road, Saffron Walden, Essex.

1963:   OC published *Movement in Two Dimensions: a study of the animated and projected pictures which preceded the invention of cinematography* (Hutchinson).

1964:   ES and OC collaborated on *British Churches* (Studio Vista).

ES collaborated with Edward Hyams on *The English Garden* (Thames & Hudson).

1965:   ES and OC collaborated on *The Wonders of Italy* (Thames & Hudson) and *Prospect of Cambridge* (Batsford).

1966:   ES and OC collaborated with Micheal Liammóir on *Ireland* (Thames & Hudson).   93
ES collaborated with A J Youngson on *The Making of Classical Edinburgh* (Edinburgh University Press).

1967:   ES and OC moved from the centre of Saffron Walden to the Coach House, Windmill Hill.

ES and OC collaborated on *The Stansted Affair: A Case for the People* (Pan Books), the culmination of their campaign against a third London airport.

ES worked as stills photographer on David Thompson's documentary film, *The Pre-Raphaelite Revolt*.

1968:   ES and OC collaborated with Eric Linklater on *Scotland* (Thames & Hudson).

1969:   ES worked as stills photographer on Dudley Shaw Ashton's documentary film, *Rembrandt's The Three Crosses*. ES published *A Small World*, a collection of his wood engravings.

1970:   ES held the only show of his photographs during his lifetime. He showed alongside the amateur, Peter Soar, at Joshua Taylor's department store, as part of the Cambridge Festival.

OC published *Ardna Gashel – An Allegory* (Golden Press), with linocuts and pattern paper by ES.

1971:   ES purchased a second-hand Linhof camera.

29 December: ES died at home, of pancreatic cancer.

1973:   A memorial exhibition of the photographs of ES was held at the Aldeburgh Festival.

1978:   OC wrote the libretto for Christopher Brown's children's opera, *The Split Goose Feather*.

1984:   OC published *Edwin Smith: Photographs 1935-1971* (Thames & Hudson).

1985:   OC was instrumental, with Iris Weaver, in helping found the Fry Art Gallery, Saffron Walden, dedicated to artists from North East Essex.

1987:   The Fry Art Gallery was opened.

1992:   OC published *Cuts: Wood & Linocuts* (Previous Parrot Press), with cuts and pattern paper by ES.

1998:   OC provided the introduction to Walter Hoyle's *To Sicily with Edward Bawden* (Previous Parrot Press), which included illustrations by ES.

1999:   OC wrote *Tryphema Pruss: The Ghost of a Great Lodge* for Walter Hoyle to llustrate (the illustrated edition was published by Previous Parrot Press).

2002:   2 May: OC died at Saffron Walden Community Hospital.

For bibliographies of publications by and about Edwin Smith, please refer to Robert Elwall, *Evocations of Place: The Photography of Edwin Smith*, London: Merrell, 2007, and – a volume to which Elwall directs the reader – Alan Powers, Ian Mackenzie-Kerr, Shawn Kolucy and Rory Young, *A View of the Cotswolds*, photographs by Edwin Smith, Risbury: Whittington Press, 2005.